Original title:
In the Garden of Verse

Copyright © 2025 Creative Arts Management OÜ
All rights reserved.

Author: Thomas Sinclair
ISBN HARDBACK: 978-1-80567-079-7
ISBN PAPERBACK: 978-1-80567-159-6

Nature's Canvas of Expression

Under the sun, the daisies dance,
With silly faces, they take their chance.
Bees buzz by with their funky tunes,
As grasshoppers hop, wearing tiny shoes.

The roses blush, like they've been told,
Secrets of love, in petals of gold.
While worms do the tango in hidden delight,
Creating a ruckus, oh what a sight!

Vignettes of Verdure

A squirrel slips on a slippery pine,
Stealing a nut, thinking it's fine.
The oak tree chuckles, leaves all aglow,
While hedgehogs giggle, putting on a show.

The tulips quip in a floral debate,
About who's the prettiest, it's hard to state.
Sunflowers stand tall, striking a pose,
While violets snicker, blushing with prose.

Whispers of a Blossoming Dream

Caterpillars wear jackets, puffing up slow,
Chasing after butterflies, putting on a show.
The daisies snicker, with their petal-tipped glee,
As the sun starts to set, painting the spree.

The lilies gossip, twirling in grace,
About a snail's race, oh what a pace!
Crickets tell riddles under the moon's glance,
While flowers all sway, joining the dance.

The Language of Petals

Down by the stream, frogs serenade night,
While fireflies waltz, bringing soft light.
Tulips tease, with whispers so sweet,
Making the daisies tap their tiny feet.

The ivy creeps closer, the ivy creeps wide,
As ladybugs giggle, they cannot hide.
With petals as pages, their stories unfold,
Oh, nature's own jester, so silly and bold!

Growing Verses in Dappled Light

Sunbeams tickle leafy heads,
As words sprout from the beds.
Tulips giggle, daisies dance,
While rhymes play hopscotch in a trance.

Butterflies wearing silly hats,
Plotting verses with fluffy cats.
Chirping birds chime in the play,
As puns grow wild, bright as the day.

Chronicles of the Earth's Palette

The soil whispers tales so bright,
As carrots dream in tones of light.
Peas in pods plot their own story,
While radishes bask in leafy glory.

A mint leaf murmurs secrets sweet,
To dill that dances on nimble feet.
Each sprout juggles meanings clear,
In a garden where giggles cheer.

The Muse Amongst the Foliage

A squirrel scribbles scripts of fun,
While mushrooms shout, "We're number one!"
Gnomes crack jokes with every sprout,
As ferns wave hands to show them out.

A bumblebee buzzed a melody,
To tickle flowers' comedy.
In every petal's light embrace,
Wit takes root in this happy place.

Prose of Pollinated Dreams

Bees buzz with rhymes upon their wings,
While blossoms giggle at crooked things.
A daisy tells jokes to the sun,
As bunnies hop, declaring, "Fun!"

Each seed shares a budding tale,
In hoots and honks, they never fail.
Nature's jesters, bright and bold,
Spin yarns of laughter, never old.

Metaphors Under Moonlight

The moon's a giant ball of cheese,
Laughing at all our silly tease.
Stars are crumbs that fall and dance,
A banquet full of chance romance.

With shadows playing hide and seek,
The flowers giggle, soft and meek.
Each whisper rustles through the leaves,
As crickets strum their nightly eves.

Beetles roll in grand parade,
While sleepy frogs serenely wade.
Nature's jokes are seen at night,
In the glow of soft moonlight.

So let your laughter echo wide,
Join the critters and their pride.
Underneath this cosmic show,
The funniest tales we all know.

Hidden Harmonies in Green

The daisies wear their sunny hats,
While squirrels share their funny chats.
In the thicket, laughter swells,
As hidden melodies it tells.

The trees are dancers, swaying free,
With branches waving, 'Come join me!'
Each rustle hides a joke or two,
In nature's laugh, we find what's true.

A patch of clovers spins a tale,
Of luck and laughter without fail.
With blooms all laughing, side by side,
In this wacky green, we confide.

So dance beneath the leafy seam,
And live a wild, whimsical dream.
For in this patch, joy grows obscene,
With hidden harmonies so keen.

A Tapestry of Nature's Lines

Nature's story stitched with care,
A patchwork quilt of jokes to share.
In every petal, a pun awaits,
With rolling laughter, it celebrates.

The wind whispers lines that tickle true,
As pine trees nod, 'We love you too!'
Each rustling leaf a playful sway,
Inviting us to join the play.

Giggling rivers rush with glee,
While frogs recite their poetry.
A tapestry both wild and free,
Woven with smiles, a tapestry.

So tread softly, hear the cheer,
There's humor here in every sphere.
In nature's lines, we find the fun,
Under the bright and warming sun.

The Serenity of Silent Stanzas

In quiet corners, secrets bloom,
Among the petals, joy finds room.
The silence hums a gentle tune,
While sunbeams dance, a happy swoon.

The buttercups rejoice in sun,
While rabbits plan their next big run.
Each leaf conceals a comical tale,
In shadows where the giggles sail.

Breezes carry whispers soft,
As butterflies flutter, twisting aloft.
In this stillness, laughter prances,
With every glance, the spirit dances.

So sit awhile and take a chance,
In silent stanzas, join the dance.
With nature's mirth wrapped all around,
In quiet peace, joy can be found.

The Workshop of Weeds

In the patch where nonsense grows,
Laughter sprouts like silly prose.
The daisies giggle, the tulips wink,
While daisies debate the color of pink.

Beneath the sun, the gnomes conspire,
To plant a rumor that's bound to inspire.
They toss around seeds of wild delight,
As garden gnomes shimmer with laughter bright.

The carrots march in silly lines,
Reciting rhymes with funny signs.
While broccoli wears a crown of cheese,
And dances with the bumblebees.

A weed waltz starts to steal the scene,
With dandelions acting like a queen.
In this wild patch, there's joy to find,
Where every plant is a clever kind.

The Ritual of Watering Words

Gather round, let's splash away,
Words for plants on a sunny day.
With every drop, meanings sprout,
As we shout what it's all about.

The watering can sings a tune,
In sync with the laughter of the afternoon.
Each phrase gets soaked, it glistens right,
Sprouting sentences in pure delight.

With each squirt, a pun can grow,
A joke blooms bright, don't you know?
Watering thoughts, we watch them swell,
In the garden of stories, all is well.

When clouds arrive, the rain joins in,
Showering in laughter, laughter wins.
Dampened dirt has never been fun,
As we play with words until we're done.

Histories Woven in Ivy

In the tangle where ivy creeps,
History whispers, secrets it keeps.
Old vines twist like a wordy tale,
Sprouting laughter that's sure to prevail.

Each leaf a memory, each strand a jest,
Woven together, they never rest.
With playful twists, the past comes alive,
In a green embrace where giggles thrive.

The ivy laughs as it climbs so high,
Quoting the clouds passing by in the sky.
Each tendril plans a mischief or two,
As history dances in shades of blue.

With each loop around the fence,
The ivy schemes with a cheeky sense.
A history lesson, but it's all a game,
In verdant humor, we forget the shame.

The Chronicle of the Cosmos in Culture

Stars hang in the garden, oh what a sight,
They giggle and tumble like it's pure delight.
With cosmos stirring like a wild brew,
Every twinkle is a punchline, it's true.

Galaxies swaying in comic design,
Asteroids rolling like jokes on a line.
Each planet spins a tale in jest,
In this cosmic garden, we're truly blessed.

Black holes giggle, sucking in the jokes,
While comets race with quirky folks.
Gravity's folly makes laughter soar,
In orbits of wit, who could ask for more?

The moon cracks jokes with a craters' glare,
While suns burst giggles in solar flare.
In the universe's plot, we're all entwined,
Where humor blooms in every mind.

Metaphors in the Meadow

Grass whispers secrets, a lighthearted tale,
Flowers wear hats made of bright, sunny ale.
Bees wear tuxedos, buzzing with cheer,
While frogs play the banjo, the music's sincere.

Clouds drift like marshmallows, fluffy and white,
The sun is a flashlight, shining so bright.
Worms wear their spectacles, reading the ground,
And daisies hold court with the best jokes around.

The trees tell the stories, their branches sway tall,
A squirrel's the jester, he's clever and small.
Grasshoppers dance, both silly and spry,
While butterflies giggle as they flutter by.

Each corner of nature has humor to share,
In the meadow of laughter, there's joy everywhere.

Stitched Together by Roots

Threads of the soil intertwine just right,
With daisies and dandelions, a colorful sight.
Rabbits wear aprons, baking with flair,
While hedgehogs enjoy afternoon tea with a bear.

The mushrooms play poker, sitting beneath trees,
While the crows gamble loudly, with odds like a breeze.
Ants march in chorus, a quirky parade,
As ladybugs hum tunes, serenading the shade.

Roots chat like old friends, sharing their dreams,
While seedlings debate life's most curious themes.
The magic of laughter in every green nook,
In this messy mosaic, each twig's like a book.

A patchwork of joys is sewn into sight,
In the realm where the earth spins with pure delight.

A Quilt of Quatrains

Stitched from the laughter of blooms that forget,
Each quatrain filled with giggles and fret.
Petunias in pajamas, ready for rest,
While sunflowers compete for the title of best.

The wind tells a joke that tickles the leaves,
And crickets recite poetry, dressed in their sleeves.
With hiccups of raindrops, the puddles erupt,
As frogs jump in rhythm, their antics corrupt.

The garden's a canvas, bright shades collide,
Where laughter and quirks can no longer hide.
A tapestry woven with charm and with cheer,
As insects orchestrate laughter quite near.

In this whimsical quilt, all nature's on stage,
A comedy show turns a leaf to a page.

The Symphony of Seasons

In spring, the jokes blossom, fresh as the dew,
With petals that giggle and skies painted blue.
Summer's a party with bright, juicy glee,
While watermelon slices try singing in key.

Autumn joins in with a rustle and crack,
Leaves dancing a jig, no signs of lack.
Pumpkins carve smiles, all orange and round,
As squirrels stockpile nuts, at laughter they're found.

Then winter arrives with a frosty chuckle,
Snowflakes throw snowballs—a playful snuggle.
Igloos of giggles dot the white landscape,
While penguins in bow ties prepare for an escape.

Each season resounds with a delightful refrain,
A symphony rippling through sunshine and rain.

Wandering Through the Floral Labyrinth

I took a stroll where flowers play,
They whispered secrets, oh what a day!
A rose wore glasses, looking so smart,
While daisies danced with a bouncy heart.

The tulips traded jokes in a band,
With laughter echoing through the land.
A daffodil said, 'Why don't we sing?'
The bees chimed in, 'We love to zing!'

A butterfly fluffed its colorful wing,
Claiming it was the true spring king.
But a caterpillar said with a grin,
'You'll be a moth before the next spin!'

So I giggled along with the blooms so bright,
In this maze of petals, oh what a sight!
With every twist, laughter flowed like a stream,
In this floral madness, we lived the dream.

Petal Poetry Under Starry Skies

Beneath the stars, the flowers conspire,
Sharing their dreams, like a cozy fire.
A poppy winked, wearing a crown,
While sunflowers swayed, trying not to frown.

'What's on your mind?' asked the lilac bold,
A tulip replied, 'I'm feeling quite old!'
But then a clover said with a cheer,
'You're only as young as your last beer!'

The nightingale laughed, perched on a stem,
Joining the chatter of our leafy gem.
'Let's paint the sky with our silly songs,
And dance till morning, it won't be long!'

So petals twirled, as the moonlight glowed,
In this raucous revelry, joy overflowed.
With verses spun from laughter and glee,
We danced under stars, just wild and free.

A Compendium of Flora and Fauna

In the book of blooms, where rhymes collide,
A cactus blushed, said, 'I tried to hide!'
But a fern exclaimed, 'We all have our quirks,
Just look at the lilies, they've got their smirks!'

From daisies' giggles to violets' sighs,
Every petal has stories, no room for lies.
A bumblebee buzzed, with quite the flair,
'What's life without honey? I'm royalty here!'

The wily weeds chimed in with a rhyme,
'We may be bothers, but we're just in our prime!'
With laughter resounding, nature's delight,
A tapestry woven, all wrongs felt so right.

So grab your pen and join in the fun,
In this book of blooms, we've only begun.
From flowers to critters, each tale does impart,
A compendium of joy, straight from the heart.

The Sanctuary of Syllables

In a hidden nook where letters grow,
Syllables blossom, putting on a show.
A geranium giggled, 'Can you believe,
I rhymed with a petunia on New Year's Eve?'

Mad rhymes fluttered, like butterflies bright,
Crafting a sanctuary of sheer delight.
Adjectives pranced, verbs shared a jest,
While nouns posed proudly, all dressed to impress.

The crafty commas, oh what a pair,
Played tag with the exclamation, full of flair.
In this sanctuary, the words took flight,
Painting the silence with colors so bright.

So come take a peek at this world anew,
Where every flower has something to do.
With laughter and whimsy, we gather right here,
In a haven of syllables, bringing us cheer.

Echoes through the Flowerbed

In the plot where daisies dance,
A worm spins tales of romance.
The sunflowers gossip, oh so bright,
While crickets croon through the night.

A bumblebee dons a silly hat,
And waltzes 'round the garden mat.
Petunias laugh at the creeping vine,
'You can't outstyle these blooms of mine!'

The carrots plot a vegetable heist,
While radishes play dice with the yeast.
The daffodils burst into song,
As the tulips say, 'You can't go wrong!'

In this patch of colorful cheer,
Nature's circus, come gather near.
With laughs and ticks and tocks galore,
The garden's laughter, forevermore.

The Rhythm of Roots

The roots below have quite the beat,
They wiggle and writhe beneath our feet.
The potatoes breakdance down in the dirt,
While onions juggle without a shirt.

The carrots march in a silly parade,
With leafy hats that never fade.
'Potato!' calls the leafy sage,
'Don't trip, it's a root rave stage!'

As the peas form a band with some style,
The radishes smile, 'Stay for a while!'
Bees twirl through a floral ballet,
While daisies shout, 'Hip hip hooray!'

So let's join in this joyous fun,
In the roots' rhythmic, warm sun.
With a giggle and dance, we'll play along,
In this rooty garden, where hearts belong.

Fragments of Floral Thought

A petal whispers, 'What's the scoop?'
'The roses say they know the loop.'
But daisies giggle, light and bright,
'We just bloom, with sheer delight!'

The violets scheme with clever glee,
'What if we sang in harmony?'
Lilies nod with elegant grace,
As daffodils photobomb the space.

With pollen jokes and nectar puns,
The garden buzzes with endless runs.
'What a riot!' the sunflowers say,
'Let's shower the world with laughs today!'

So here's to blooms, and chatter so free,
In fragments, we find our jubilee.
With every chuckle, sprout, and cheer,
The garden thrives, year after year.

Verdant Dreams in Rhyme

In hues of green where crickets play,
The lettuce giggles in a quirky way.
The garden spins wild tales at dusk,
Of cheeky critters, and a fragrant musk.

Basil dreams of pasta nights,
While mint concocts cool summer delights.
'Hey parsley,' shouts the thyme with flair,
'Your flavor's great, but don't lose your hair!'

The pumpkins boast of grand designs,
As squash sit plotting pranks and lines.
A chive jokes, 'It's time to rise!'
With laughter echoing through the skies.

So come and stroll this verdant place,
Where greenery wears a playful face.
With fun and whimsy intertwined,
In dreams of nature, joy we find.

Whispers in the Winter Garden

Snowflakes dance on chilly air,
Squirrels chatter, unaware.
A rabbit hops with such delight,
Wonders what to do tonight.

Frosty breath in puddles clear,
Vegetables have disappeared.
Carrots cloaked in snowy sheets,
The garden's lost its proper treats.

Jokes made by the frosty trees,
Tickling branches in the breeze.
A funny hat on every shrub,
Winter's laughter, what a hub!

Yet beneath that snowy dome,
Tiny sprouts may find their home.
With a chuckle, spring will say,
"Just you wait, I'm on my way!"

Flourishes of the Four Seasons

Spring arrives with much to say,
Buds are popping every way.
Flowers giggle, colors pop,
"Who needs winter? Let's not stop!"

Summer laughs with sunny rays,
Ants throw parties, spend their days.
Ice cream drips on sunny cheeks,
"Life is good!" the garden speaks.

Autumn twirls in golden leaves,
Dancing 'round like carefree thieves.
Pumpkins posing, all so round,
Harvest jokes abound, confound.

Winter shivers, time to cheer,
Blanket white, not one more deer.
With a wink, it takes its bow,
Seasons joke, "Let's start now!"

The Artistry of Unfurling Ferns

Ferns unfurl with grace and style,
Twisting gently all the while.
"Look at me," they laugh and tease,
"I can dance, I'm quite the breeze!"

In the shade where soft winds play,
They whisper secrets, come what may.
"Who needs sunlight?" they confer,
"Let's paint the darkness, oh dear fern!"

With each curl, they swirl and sway,
Making patterns, come what may.
"I'm not shy," one ferns says,
"Just waiting for the praise, I guess!"

Artful green, with tales to tell,
In each nook, they weave their spell.
"Let's not take ourselves so serious,
Life's much better when it's curious!"

Messages Carved in Bark

Trees stand tall with something new,
Carved initials, hearts askew.
"Who needs paper?" they all sigh,
"Nature's canvas, oh my, my!"

Bark inscriptions, tales of old,
Whisper secrets, soft and bold.
"Rabbits wed, bees on a spree,
Nature's love, just wait and see!"

Ferocious winds can't steal their laughs,
Groves of stories, photographs.
"Snap a pic?" the branches jest,
"Growing old? We're just the best!"

So if you wander, stop a while,
Listen close, the trees can smile.
"Life's a giggle, grab a snack,
Leave your worries, don't look back!"

Mapping the Metaphors

Words sprout like daisies, so they say,
But then again, some just fade away.
I planted a pun, it grew so tall,
Now it's a joke that won't stop at all.

Synonyms dance in a wild waltz,
While adverbs twirl without a fault.
Nouns hide in the shade, giggling loud,
As commas just sigh, feeling quite proud.

Verbs race by, trying not to trip,
They're fueled by coffee in a fluid sip.
Imagery blooms with colors so bright,
Painting the page in chaotic delight.

In this patch of phrases, we tend with care,
Pruning the lines and trimming the spare.
So grab your shovel, let's dig in deep,
For laughter in language, we joyfully reap.

Timelessness in Tanglewood

A tree with wise eyes stands quite still,
Watching the antics that give it a thrill.
Squirrels exchange comedic glances,
As leaves play hide and seek with their dances.

The wind whispers secrets of old,
As blooms giggle, their petals unfold.
Time ticks on, but here it's a jest,
Where days blend together, never a quest.

Clouds drift lazily, wearing a grin,
With shadows that tease where the fun might begin.
An owl hoots laughter from high above,
In a world where each moment fits like a glove.

So let's take a stroll through this playful wood,
Where nonsense and laughter always feel good.
Every branch tells a joke, every root a pun,
In timeless tomfoolery, we all weigh a ton.

The Quiet Ballad of Brambles

Brambles sing softly in the cool shade,
Whispering secrets in a messy braid.
They tickle your ankles, beg you to stay,
While thorns share the punchline in their brambly way.

Bumbling bees buzz with laughter and glee,
Wondering who'll dance next, you or me.
Petals blush pink, with jokes on their tips,
While the grass rolls around, doing little flips.

In this tangled embrace, we trip and we laugh,
Nature's own playground, the perfect gaffe.
With laughter like dew upon every leaf,
Here's a heartwarming giggle, beyond belief.

So join in the chorus of rustling green,
Where every snag tells a tale unforeseen.
As brambles confess in a melodious way,
Life's better with humor at the end of the day.

Prose from the Pruning Shears

Pruning shears chatters, snipping away,
Muttering tales of the bushy ballet.
With a snip-snap here and a clip-clip there,
They gossip of growth in the Botanical Fair.

Accurate angles with a twist of a branch,
As tufts of grass giggle and prance.
Roses pretend they're shy with their blush,
While weeds crack jokes in the final hush.

Each cut—a punchline, sharp and sincere,
Crafting a garden that's void of all fear.
With every straight line, a character grows,
Adding some laughter wherever it goes.

So lend me your ear, and snip with delight,
For prose from the shears brings the day into light.
In this playful patch, we'll edit with glee,
As we cultivate humor in green jubilee.

Imagery in Bloom

Petunias in puns play around,
Tulips giggle, arms unbound.
Marigolds dance, a silly twist,
Garden gnomes join in, can't resist.

Butterflies wear silly hats,
While bumblebees prefer their bats.
Every stem tells a joke or two,
Laughter blooms, in every hue.

Lettuce wraps a comical tale,
As carrots flaunt their vibrant veil.
Beets are bashful, turn to red,
But they too, joke when they're fed.

Chopped herbs whisper cheeky rhymes,
While twirling vines keep perfect times.
Nature's stage where mirth arises,
In the soil, humor never disguises.

Musings by the Garden Gate

At the threshold, laughter waits,
Worms wiggle in their garden states.
A lettuce leaf, a wise old sage,
Cracks jokes that never age.

Birds exchange their chirpy quips,
While daisies shake their sunny hips.
The fence once splintered, now delighted,
With tales of weeds, they feel inspired.

A squirrel juggles acorns bright,
While shadows dance in morning light.
Roses blush at jokes so free,
Buzzing bees hum harmony.

Pines whisper secrets in the breeze,
Bubbling pools laugh with such ease.
By the gate, oh what a sight,
Humor thrums from morn to night.

Lyrical Shadows of Sunflowers

Tall and proud with a silly grin,
Sunflowers sway, let the fun begin.
Their heads held high, they nod in cheer,
Tickling the clouds that linger near.

Petals spin tales of summer days,
With sunlit laughter in golden rays.
They giggle with the buzzing bees,
And whisper at the passing breeze.

Lurking behind, a shadow's joke,
Dandelions tease with a cheeky poke.
Each seed a mischief-making spark,
As the garden hums in the dark.

Their laughter trails through dusk's embrace,
As moonlight paints a happy face.
In the shadows, brilliance glows,
Where the garden's humor freely flows.

The Harmonies of Hand-Tilled Earth

With spade in hand, I hum along,
The soil sings a merry song.
Each turn unearths a comedy,
As worms perform their symphony.

Weeds play tricks upon the rows,
Root-tangled giggles nobody knows.
While cabbages hold a judgmental stare,
Lettuce laughs without a care.

Compost heaps share wisecracks low,
As rain droplets join the show.
Tilling tunes of nature's best,
In earthy rhythms, hilarity's quest.

At harvest time, the laughter swells,
With every carrot, a tale that tells.
Hand-tilled earth, a quirky scene,
Where humor sprouts evergreen.

Cacophony of the Bumblebee

A bumblebee buzzes, wearing a hat,
With pollen-filled pockets, imagine that!
He dances on petals, a clumsy ballet,
While flowers all giggle, "No buzz off, we say!"

He trips on a daisy, oh what a clatter,
Swatting at flies, all flustered and fatter.
The garden erupts in a raucous delight,
As he spins in the air, then lands with a fright.

A ladybug chuckles from high on a leaf,
Dropping her sidekick, the mischief-prone beef.
The roses are snickering, the tulips partake,
At the bumblebee's antics, they giggle awake.

With each little stumble, the flowers all cheer,
Our buzzing friend brings a silly good cheer.
So let's raise a toast, with dew on the grass,
To the bumblebee blunders that never shall pass!

The Rhyme of Trampled Thorns

Once I tiptoed barefoot through a patch of despair,
Tripped on some thorns—what a sight! I swear!
The roses stood tall, with a smirk on their face,
Saying, "Here comes the gardener, oh what a race!"

I shuffled and stumbled, a sight most absurd,
A ballet of panic, I barely could herd.
The daisies were laughing, the violets in glee,
As I danced like a fool, 'neath the bough of a tree.

But the thorns held their ground, they raised up their heads,
"You trampled our beauty, now get out of beds!"
I promised to watch where my clumsy feet roam,
But we all know the garden won't leave me alone!

So I tiptoe and shuffle, a new kind of grace,
In a world full of laughter, I find my own place.
With a grin on my lips, and some poke in my toes,
You'll find funny tales in the flowerbed rows!

Choices Among the Colorful Weeds

In a patch of wild color, the weeds have a chat,
"Hey, I'm growing taller, what do you think of that?"
One flaunts a bright yellow, another a fright,
"Who's the queen of this garden? Let's argue tonight!"

The daisies rolled eyes, nearly fell off their stems,
"You're just wild nonsense, you're adding to phlegms!"
The violets chimed in, quite sweet, I must say,
"We don't want your drama, please go play away!"

But the weeds didn't budge, full of laughter and sass,
"As if any flower could ever surpass!"
They tangled their roots in a root-tango spree,
While the flowers just groaned, "Oh please let us be!"

So celebrate choices, both humble and bold,
As weeds find their power, let their stories unfold.
In the clash of the petals, a twist weaves its thread,
The garden bursts open, with laughter instead!

Verses Written in Phlox

In fields where phlox chatter, a poetry jam,
They rhyme 'bout the gardeners, oh what a sham!
With polka-dot petals and a flair for the fun,
They wrangle their verses, like a game of whun.

"Oh look at that fellow, with his watering can!"
The phlox do declare, as they fan and they plan.
"He thinks he's a poet, with his sprinkle and squirt,
But all he can grow is a pile of old dirt!"

With a flick of their colors, they puff and they preen,
Making rhymes about bugs, oh what a scene!
A ladybug joins in, with a tap on a tune,
And the garden erupts in this whimsical boon.

So join us in laughter, where the colors ignite,
As verses dance freely, a joyful delight.
In this phlox-scented world, every whisper is clever,
With humor in petals, we'll bloom on forever!

Blooming Words of Serenity

Words sprout like daisies, so bright,
Whispers of joy take flight.
Laughter dances on each page,
As puns play on—what a stage!

In this patch of playful prose,
Where silly thoughts take their doze.
A giggle blooms with every line,
Even the rhymes are feeling fine.

Petals of jokes unfurl with glee,
As metaphors jump like bees.
In this bright and funny glade,
Every pun's a blooming cascade.

So come, let's sip on verse today,
Where laughter grows in every way.
Each line a flower, bold and free,
In this garden of fricassee!

The Language of Leaves

Leaves gossip softly in the breeze,
Telling tales that tickle knees.
A rustle here, a chuckle there,
Nature's jokes are everywhere!

Caterpillars wear fancy hats,
While bumblebees have chatty spats.
The sun peeks in, a cheeky clown,
As shadows shrug their leafy gowns.

Each twig holds secrets, whispers fun,
As squirrels dance and jump and run.
The trees have words—oh, what a tease,
In languages that aim to please!

With every sway, laughter's shared,
In this leafy world, none are scared.
So join the chortles, let them soar,
In this delightful, leafy lore!

Rhymes on the Breeze

Rhymes float gently through the air,
Teasing birds with flair and dare.
A playful breeze, a giggly sprite,
Turns each line into pure delight.

Clouds chuckle with a fluffy grin,
As jokers dance and whirl within.
Nature hums a merry tune,
Beneath the light of a silvery moon.

From flowers' lips, the verses spring,
As happy thoughts take flight on wings.
Every rhyme, a tickle to share,
Breath of laughter everywhere.

So join the breeze, let laughter flow,
In this ballet of rhythm's glow.
Each word a seed, sprouting free,
As humor blooms eternally!

Sonnets of Sunlit Shadows

Shadows play in sunlight's glow,
Making shapes that dance and flow.
Each line a twist, a funny frame,
In the game of silly fame.

Beneath tall trees, the sunlight laughs,
As squirrels check their funny graphs.
Every shadow finds its rhyme,
In this playful, sunny clime.

A poet's pen, a winking star,
Sprinkles joy both near and far.
The sonnets tease, they spin and twirl,
In the tapestry of laughter's whirl.

So come, dear friend, take a seat,
Join this party of rhythm and beat.
Each sonnet, a bright, jovial show,
In the realm where funny shadows grow!

Fragments from the Floral Archive

Petunias gossip, oh what a sight,
Tulips sharing tales late at night.
Daisies dancing, full of glee,
Roses rolling in a raucous spree.

Violets whisper secrets sweet,
While pansies prance on nimble feet.
A sunflower trying to play the clown,
Wobbling about, almost falls down.

Marigolds giggle, looking so bright,
Cacti chuckle, with all their might.
A daffodil dreams of a happy waltz,
While every petal exclaims, "No faults!"

Blooming laughter fills the air,
Nature's jokes everywhere.
The fragrant verses of this spree,
Bring smiles to all, especially me.

Phrases Floating on the Breeze

Butterflies chat in shades of blue,
While dandelions laugh, oh so true.
A bumblebee hums a silly tune,
As daisies join in, beneath the moon.

Lilies giggle, all dressed in white,
Blushing roses blush with delight.
Petals flutter, tales they weave,
As bees buzz on, they hardly leave.

A garden gnome grins, cheeky and sly,
Waving to passersby with a winked eye.
Laughter's the air, like a bouquet,
Why do we rake when we can play?

Wishes wander on the breeze,
Tickling petals with gentle ease.
In this patch of grounded cheer,
Joy blooms brightly, year after year.

Illuminated by Moonlit Blooms

Daisies shine under the moon's soft glow,
Nightshade whispers secrets, just so.
Crickets croak jokes, some wise, some odd,
As cosmos twirl, a dance with God.

A rose in pajamas, snoring aloud,
While tulips throw a midnight crowd.
Laughter echoes through silvery beams,
As petals hatch their wildest dreams.

Foxgloves giggle, dressed to impress,
While nightingales sing, oh what a mess!
Gladiolus tries to impress a bee,
But trips on its own feet, oh dear me!

Starlit giggles fill the plot,
Nature's jesters, quite a lot.
In this bouquet of whims and cheer,
Every creature holds laughter dear.

The Ink of Insects in Motion

Ladybugs sketch with their tiny pens,
Writing stories that never ends.
Grasshoppers leap, bound with delight,
Creating cartoons under moonlight.

Ants put on plays, quite the display,
As they march and dance, in their own way.
A caterpillar juggles with ease,
While beetles join in, beg for a breeze.

Worms scribble sonnets in soft, cool dirt,
With every word, they giggle and flirt.
Spider spins tales with threads of pure gold,
A tapestry rich, with laughter sold.

In this garden, where whimsy is king,
Insects create, flutter, and sing.
With each little buzz, a rhyme in the air,
In the garden of laughter, we banish despair.

The Allure of the Collected Critters

A butterfly landed, oh what a sight,
It posed and it preened, in morning light.
A ladybug giggled, wearing her dots,
While ants held a meeting on cookie plots.

A worm told a joke, though it was quite neat,
About how he wriggled to a funky beat.
Grasshoppers chuckled, leaping with glee,
As bees buzzed along, sipping sweet tea.

The beetles were dancing, all in a row,
With moves so absurd, it stole the show.
A cricket recited some terrible rhymes,
But the audience cheered, loving his crimes.

So here's to the critters, all funny and small,
In a world full of laughter, they welcome us all.
With wings, and with legs, and a shimmer of cheer,
Together they sparkle, bringing us near.

The Melancholy of Dried Blooms

Oh wilted petals, sad as can be,
Once vibrant and lively, now sighing for glee.
They reminisce whispers of sunlit days,
While collecting dust in sepia haze.

The violets frown, their purple turned grey,
As they envy new buds that bask in the play.
The roses compare their crumbles and curls,
To happy fresh flowers in nearby swirls.

A daisy complained, 'I'm not feeling bright!'
'Just look at us now, we were quite a sight!'
Yet, laughter erupts from stems stiff and torn,
For dried blooms can chuckle on frosty morn.

So here in this moment, we pause and we stare,
At the beauty of blossoms that once had great flair.
Though faded and funny, they dance in despair,
A quirky reminder that life's never fair.

A Sonnet in the Shadows

Under the canopy, critters conspire,
To share all the gossip from here to the mire.
A spider spins tales of tragedy most grand,
While fireflies flicker, with jokes well-planned.

The hedgehog just snorted, puffed up in delight,
Listening closely to whispers of night.
A moth flits around, all dressed up to play,
While owls hoot humor in mysterious ways.

The shadows hide secrets, both funny and bright,
As darkness wraps softly, cloaking the light.
But laughter escapes in a twinkling glow,
With every little critter, putting on a show.

So revel in moments where giggles reside,
In whispers of shadows where joys often hide.
For even the dusk has a chuckle to lend,
In the souls of the creatures, laughter won't end.

The Palette of the Pollinator

Bees paint the air with sweet melodies,
Rouge petals blush as they flutter with ease.
A butterfly giggles, adorned in her dress,
As she tickles the blooms in a sunny caress.

The hummingbird hovers, a jewel in flight,
With a buzz and a twirl, he's a marvelous sight.
A painted lady chuckles, 'Oh what a scene!'
As colors collide in a bright vibrant sheen.

From lilac to lemon, each petal a hue,
They mingle and dance with the morning dew.
The color wheel spins, with pollen to share,
In a raucous fiesta, they giggle in air.

So raise up your glasses, to nature's great show,
To the palette of pollinators, putting on a glow.
For in this bright garden, where laughter ignites,
It's the zany little creatures that bring pure delight.

Nature's Lullaby in Staccato

Butterfly dreams in a tea cup,
A worm wears a hat, feels like a pup,
Bees buzz a tune, oh what a sight,
While daisies chat late into the night.

Chirp of the crickets, a jig in the grass,
Silly old toads use the pond as their class,
A frog takes a leap, but lands on a snail,
While grasshoppers giggle at the slip of the tail.

Squirrels wear glasses, flipping through pages,
Reading the news of the stars and their sages,
The trees laugh softly, their shadows they cast,
As the sun goes to bed, the giggles are vast.

Night wraps its arms, all snug and tight,
With twinkling stars winking like they might,
Nature's own lullaby, funny and bright,
Sings to the critters till the morning light.

Syllables and Seeds

Seeds take a tumble, dance in the air,
While ants roll their ball with a desperate flair,
Each syllable giggles, a rhyme on the breeze,
As flowers join in with the rustling leaves.

The sun sneezes once, then squirts out a ray,
While daisies discuss their plans for the day,
A beetle goes roller-skating down a leaf,
Claiming it's all just a tale beyond belief.

Worms in a circle, they plot and they scheme,
Stitching up dreams with a leafy seam,
Every petal whispers, a joke here and there,
Nature's own comedy, floating through air.

The moon rolls its eyes, shakes its bright head,
As flowers tell tales of their delicate spread,
With laughs drifting softly like clouds high above,
Syllables and seeds, all chatting of love.

The Harmony of Earth and Ink

Ink spills like rain on a paper made leaf,
Words sprout like flowers, causing much grief,
A daisy speaks in a language so fine,
While a sparrow critiques every crooked line.

The ground chuckles softly, dirt in its grin,
As pebbles gossip, "Let the fun begin!"
Hummingbirds hover, writing notes on the fly,
Each stanza a flight, leaping high to the sky.

Pencils turn green, with envy and joy,
While worms become poets, oh what a ploy!
The roots drink the verses, sip with delight,
In a show full of giggles, from morning to night.

Together, they dance, this quirky brigade,
With paper and petals, a whimsical trade,
The harmony flows, like a river of ink,
Where earth meets the words, in a silly wink.

Inked Imagery in Blossom

With brush strokes of laughter, petals unfold,
Every petal giggles, each story told,
The ink spills and dances across every stem,
As bees pollinate puns from a well-aged gem.

Twigs tap their toes while the blossoms sway,
Composing a tune in a light-hearted way,
The sun grins wide, casting shadows of fun,
As creatures compose their own songs in the sun.

A snail pens a letter to a wandering breeze,
Scribbling sweet nothings to tease and to please,
The garden erupts, with color and quip,
As every inked image takes a joyful trip.

In whispered tones, the flowers do bloom,
Painting the world with their jovial plume,
With every chuckle, a new rhyme takes flight,
Inked imagery swirls, a colorful sight.

The Celestial Orchard

Beneath a tree, a squirrel did prance,
He tried to dance, but just took a chance.
He slipped on an apple, such a bold feat,
And landed right on a gardener's seat.

The bees were buzzing, wearing their ties,
Planning a ball, much to my surprise.
With tiny tuxedos and hats so tall,
They bopped and wiggled, a buzzing ball!

The moonlit nights brought odd friends to toast,
A cactus and gopher, who both loved to boast.
They shared their secrets, like who was more prickly,
While laughing so hard, the shadows danced sickly.

Yet when dawn broke, they scattered away,
Leaving behind their laughter at play.
For in this orchard, every day's grand,
With laughter and mischief, all perfectly planned.

Fables of Fern and Frangipani

Once a fern, with fronds so green,
Wished to be a flower, fit for a queen.
Frangipani laughed, with petals bright,
"You dance in the breeze, that's pure delight!"

They summoned the sun, a charismatic dude,
Who wore shades and cooked up some food.
"Let's have a feast!" he bellowed with glee,
Where ferns told tales and danced with a bee.

The grasshoppers chirped, their legs in sync,
Missed the point of the fresh lemonade drink.
While sipping the nectar, they sang quite absurd,
With each silly note, the garden concurred!

In the end, the fern shone in its own way,
Realized fun's the brightest bouquet.
No matter the height, or color, or stance,
Life's all about joy, not just a chance.

Poetry in the Pollen

In a field of daisies, a poet sneezed,
Each puff was a stanza, oh how he pleased!
The flowers then giggled, tickled by air,
As rhymes floated off, like perfume in fair.

Butterflies waltzed in a lyrical trance,
While ants held a meeting to plot their next dance.
Every line sprouted wings, how they took flight,
Sipping on nectar, until late in the night.

A ladybug chimed in with a tune,
Her spots were her notes, in dark or in moon.
While worms composed verses all snug in their dirt,
Chasing their dreams, and not a moment of hurt.

Though silly and light, their verses were grand,
A symphony echoed across the vast land.
In pollen they found their jubilant threads,
Sprinkling laughter as day turned to beds.

Rhymes of Rooted Realities

On a root so deep, came a frog with a hat,
"Good day!" he croaked with a flair and a spat.
Every word was a riddle, wrapped up in green,
While worms in the soil just giggled unseen.

A dandelion swayed, proclaiming with pride,
"I'm the true king, let the sunshine be my guide!"
But the daisies just laughed, with their petals in style,
"There's more to this garden than just your green smile!"

As pickle jars sang, in the pantry nearby,
They dreamed of a picnic under the sky.
With sandwiches dancing, and cupcakes that prance,
Who knew that veggies could innovate dance?

So here's to the roots, the worms, and the cheer,
In tinfoil caps, we'll celebrate here.
For laughter and troubles, we'll share as we rhyme,
In a garden of whimsy, one verse at a time.

Stanzas Amidst the Vines

A snail once wore a tiny hat,
He thought he looked quite dapper, just like a diplomat.
But as he crawled, he lost his way,
And bumped into a tree—oh, what a fray!

The vine said, "Hey there, friend, take it slow!"
But the snail just laughed, "I'm the fastest you know!"
With goals so high and plans so grand,
He raced to the top but fell flat on the sand.

In the grape's great shade, he had quite a feast,
Chasing after dreams, he became quite the beast!
But soon he snoozed, no dreams to chase,
Just visions of grapes, in his happy place.

So if you see a snail with a dream to chase,
Don't rush him along; he's still finding his pace!
Life's not a sprint but a giggling race,
Let's all wear hats—if only for grace!

Rhythms of the Wildflower

A dandelion danced when the breeze blew near,
It twirled through the fields with no worry or fear.
"I'm not just a weed with a puffball of fluff!"
"I'm a wildflower queen, and I've got the right stuff!"

The butterflies giggled, gave her quite the cheer,
As she twinkled in sunlight, the season's debutante here.
"Look at me strut! I'm blooming with flair!"
But tripped on a root—oh, such a despair!

The bees buzzed in laughter, enjoying the show,
As our flower got up, with a flamboyant glow.
"Who cares if I stumble? I'm still full of style!"
"In this vibrant garden, I'll dance and beguile!"

So take a lesson from a dandelion bright,
Fall flat on your face, then get up with delight.
Embrace all your quirks, in your own funky way,
Bloom wildly, my friends; chase the clouds away!

Poetry Beneath the Willow

Under a willow with branches so long,
Squirrels were gathered, plotting a song.
They formed a band with nuts and a twig,
Performing 'Nutcracker Suite'—wrapped up in their gig!

The rabbits hopped in, they couldn't resist,
"Can we be backup? We won't be missed!"
So they took a bow, some wobbly and wise,
Turning the stage into laughter and sighs.

But just then appeared a pigeon so bold,
Claimed it was time for a "Squirrelish" scold.
"You can't play here; this is my turf!"
But the squirrels just laughed, "You've lost your worth!"

With a flip of a tail and a thump of a drum,
They played on until the sun went numb.
Grumpy pigeons and bunnies adored,
Embracing the silliness they all adored!

Verses Among the Blossoms

A bumblebee buzzed, with a flower to woo,
"Oh darling, I think it's just me and you!"
But the rose just chuckled, "You're quite the charmer,
But I'm getting old—you should look for a warmer!"

The bee, undeterred, went on with great flair,
"I'll bring you a nectar—a perfect love affair!"
He danced and he twirled, all through the bloom,
But a gust of wind sent him flying—from gloom!

He landed on daisies, and oh what a sight!
"Why chase a rose, when daisies are right?"
To have a good laugh, or to land a sweet kiss,
Forget the fancy flowers—this is pure bliss!

So if your love life is buzzing with dread,
Remember those daisies, not roses instead!
The best of blooms come without a fuss,
Just dance on the breeze, and enjoy the buzz!

Rhythms of the Rolling Hills

I planted my socks under a tree,
Hoping they'd grow into shoes for me.
But alas, they just lay there, flat,
While birds laughed, 'Oh, what's up with that?'

The carrots talk gossip, oh so sly,
While cabbages plot how to fly high.
In a world where veggies take flight,
I'm just waiting for my toast to ignite!

There's a dog who thinks he's a cat,
Chasing his tail - oh, what's up with that?
He leaps through the petals with joyful sound,
While I just hope the weeds stay down.

Butterflies dance on a wobbly beam,
While ants march on, like a soldier's team.
They giggle and chat without a care,
In a nature circus, oh, isn't it rare?

Verses at Twilight's Door

The stars are winking, oh what a sight,
As squirrels prepare for their nightly flight.
One even buzzes, thinking he's a bee,
I chuckle aloud, what a sight to see!

A rabbit in boots hops by with flair,
With daisies in hand, he takes to the air.
He twirls and he spins, all in the glow,
While I just ponder which way to go.

The tomatoes, they giggle, swaying with glee,
While the old pumpkin grumbles, 'Let me be free!'
They plot a parade, more fun than the last,
Now it's time to see how long they can last.

As night blankets all with a fluffy embrace,
Each flower is dreaming, a smile on its face.
I whisper a secret, just us tonight,
As the moon beams chuckle, so charmingly bright.

Petal-soft Portrayals

A daisy declared it was wiser than thyme,
While violets burst out in poetic rhyme.
"Oh, sweet dears," said the rhubarb with pride,
"Let's crown the best flower, and let's not bide!"

A rose in a tutu attempted to twirl,
But ended up dancing with dirt in a whirl.
With laughter erupting, the daisies took flight,
As the sun peeked in with its morning light.

Sunflowers whispering sweet nothings for fun,
Arguing politely who's the tallest one.
With cocky grins, they stretch up so high,
While I pluck a weed, and my spirits just fly.

In this quirky garden, mischief's the king,
Where herbs throw a party and flowers can sing.
I join in the fun, dancing barefoot with glee,
As magic unfolds, just my plants and me.

The Melody of Charmed Growth

There's a frog with a banjo, singing a tune,
'That's not for the garden, you silly goon!'
But the petals are clapping like fans in a show,
As the pond serenades the soft evening glow.

Dandelions giggle, as children will pick,
Saying, 'Make a wish,' but it's just a fun trick.
With dreams in their pockets, they scatter the seeds,
While caterpillars plot to compete in their deeds.

A shady old oak grumbles, 'My branches are sore!'
While grasshoppers tease him, 'Just take it more core!'
But the winds keep on whispering sweet melodies,
As the garden just sways with the hum of the bees.

In this cacophony of laughs and of cheer,
The flowers are giggling, and not one shows fear.
For in this chaotic, whimsical show,
The beauty of nature continues to grow.

www.ingramcontent.com/pod-product-compliance
Lightning Source LLC
Chambersburg PA
CBHW071813160426
43209CB00003B/74